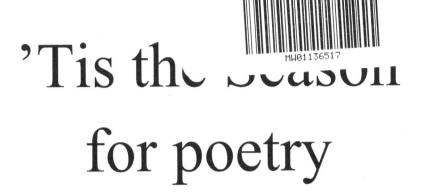

'Tis the Season

for poetry

Through the year with poems and activities
for children and their families

by Kari Vanhoozer

Illustrated by Andrew, Samuel, and
Olivia Grace Vanhoozer

Good Books Publisher

ISBN: 978-0-578-78399-4

Cover design by: Olivia Grace Vanhoozer
Library of Congress Control Number: 2018675309
Printed in the United States of America

I dedicate this book to my Spring Baby, Katelyn.

Finally, brethren, whatsoever things are true, whatsoever things are honest, whatsoever things are just, whatsoever things are pure, whatsoever things are lovely, whatsoever things are of good report; if there be any virtue, and if there be any praise, think on these things. Philippians 4:8

Table of Contents

Introduction

It started with Daffodils. My-three-year-old and I were walking in the neighborhood in early spring and saw the tall, yellow flowers. I immediately recited in sing-song rhythm

> I wandered lonely as a cloud
> That floats on high o'er vales and hills,
> When all at once I saw a crowd,
> A host, of golden daffodils;
> Beside the lake, beneath the trees,
> Fluttering and dancing in the breeze.

This was the beginning of the only poem I was ever asked to memorize in all my schooling. I am grateful to the venerable English Literature professor at Baylor University, Dr. Wortman, for requiring me to learn this poem by heart. For, it came out of my heart when I needed it.

As I added children to our homeschooling family, I added poems, rhymes, Bible verses, hymns, prayers and speeches to our memory work that related to the season or day in history. Older children would add mature poems and passages to their own repertoire. Sometimes, I maximized these relevant moments with art, copy-work, and research. I chose poems with subjects that, when seen or celebrated, would remind us to recite the memory work we had learned as a family.

The collection of writings in your hands took us over a decade to read or memorize; often we learned one new poem each season. You may choose to delight in these words much faster: the book's format is organized so you have a poem for each week of each month of one year.

How to Read

Read aloud the poems to your children: in the morning to awaken them or at bedtime to relax them, or after lunch or at afternoon snack while all are still gathered. As you read, pause at the rhyming words; if the poem does not rhyme, pause at the punctuation, not at the end of the line. Reading the poem can be enough. Or, you can spend more time with each writing as a unit study with many teachable moments like finding the author's home on a map or reading a biography or encyclopedia entry about the subject, and then having your child narrate to you while you record their words. This dictation can be added to their timeline: a binder of people and events ordered chronologically, but not learned about chronologically. All reading aloud builds your children's vocabulary, strengthens bonds between family members, and provides common poems among all of you. Use the blank spaces under each month separating the parts of the book to write down related books, activities or poems you find elsewhere that you would like to read a fifth week of a month or another year. The season is listed to remind you that many of the poems can easily be read anytime during the given season.

How to Memorize

Some writings are worth knowing by heart. This is eased by mom or dad knowing the words themselves or keeping the words before them to aid the family in remembering as you walk about your day. Younger children can memorize short poems that will be inspired for recitation upon seeing the subject in real life, such as rain, squirrels, and daffodils. Older children can memorize a whole, long poem. Younger children can memorize one stanza of a larger poem. That can be enough, or each year you can add a stanza (as my children did for "I Wandered Lonely as a Cloud") until the whole poem is learned by heart.

Speak the poem aloud in phrases to allow time for your children to echo your words. For younger children and shorter poems, this ongoing method is sufficient. For older children follow one step each day:

1. Mom speaks and children echo repeatedly
2. Children copy poem in writing
3. Mom dictates to children while they write
4. Children write from memory (may take multiple days)
5. Children recite by heart.

Bookmark Maker
and Card Art Maker and Copy Work

To keep the words before our eyes, my children make bookmarks. We cut cardstock to size, write the poem and add related art. Variations: round the corners, punch holes for tassels, glue a typed poem if too long. We like to use a paper cutter designed for crafters to cut straight lines. Our preferred mediums are colored pencils (Prismacolor brand) and water colors (Prang brand). Additional supplies we keep in our kit: waterproof markers, crayons for watercolor resist, and markers (when all the children are aged). Similarly we make greeting cards with blank cardstock and matching envelope kits. The art will be shown on the front and the poem will be written on the back. If the children are young, I will write the poem (or a stanza of the poem) in light pencil for the children to trace; afterwards, I erase the pencil lines. With original art and memorable verse, the cards get sent away to cheer the recipients as we thank them or wish them birthday greetings.

January

Winter

North wind doth blow

By Mother Goose
England, 16th century

The north wind doth blow,
And we shall have snow,
And what will the robin do then, poor thing?
He'll sit in a barn,
And keep himself warm,
And hide his head under his wing, poor thing!

The north wind doth blow,
And we shall have snow,
And what will the swallow do then, poor thing?
Oh, do you not know
That he's off long ago
To a country where he'll find spring, poor thing!

The north wind doth blow,
And we shall have snow,
And what will the dormouse do then, poor thing?
Roll'd up like a ball,
In his nest snug and small,
He'll sleep till warm weather comes in, poor thing!

The north wind doth blow,
And we shall have snow,
And what will the honey-bee do then, poor thing?
In his hive he will stay
Till the cold is away,
And then he'll come out in the spring, poor thing!

(continued)

The north wind doth blow,
And we shall have snow,
And what will the children do then, poor things?
When lessons are done,
They must skip, jump and run,
Until they have made themselves warm, poor things!

Notes

Read this poem with a lyrical, sing-voice, pausing at the rhyming words and also at the punctuation.

Art: https://artprojectsforkids.org/paint-a-snowman/ draw the snowman with pencil, then trace in ink, erase pencil lines, draw wind swirls with a white crayon or oil pastel, then paint with watercolors. We replaced the yellow bird in the tutorial with a robin to match the poem.

Our interest in this poem led us to read the well-illustrated book *Nick Butterworth's Book of Nursery Rhymes,* and it is from this book that my young daughter chose the two stanzas that meant the most to her to learn by heart. Our bookmark kept our place daily in our McGuffey's reader all winter long.

Books: *The Long Winter* by Laura Ingalls Wilder (reads aloud well), *Winter Story* by Jill Barklem (personification), *The Big Snow* by Berta and Elmer Hader (relates how the animals prepare for winter)

Snow

By Anonymous

The Snow fell softly all the night.
It made a blanket soft and white.
It covered houses, flowers, and ground.
But did not make a single sound.

Notes

The word "anonymous" comes from a Greek word that means "without a name". We use the word Anonymous when we do not know who wrote a poem.

Art: Winter scene of snow with fence line, cardinal, snow falling (use cotton swab or pinky finger). Talk about foreground, middle ground, and background before painting the layers. Very satisfying to ages 12-18. Example on cover has acrylic craft paint; mix white or black into blue paint to get varying shades.

Books: *Snow is Falling* by Franklin Branley (from Let's-Read-and-Find-Out Science series), *Snowflake Bentley* by Jacqueline Martin, and *White Snow, Bright Snow* by Alvin Tresselt.

Twinkle, Twinkle, Little Star

By Jane Taylor
England, 1806

Twinkle, twinkle, little star,
How I wonder what you are!
Up above the world so high,
Like a diamond in the sky.

When the blazing sun is gone,
When he nothing shines upon,
Then you show your little light,
Twinkle, twinkle, all the night.

Then the trav'ller in the dark,
Thanks you for your tiny spark,
He could not see which way to go,
If you did not twinkle so.

In the dark blue sky you keep,
And often thro' my curtains peep,
For you never shut your eye,
Till the sun is in the sky.

'Tis your bright and tiny spark,
Lights the trav'ller in the dark,
Tho' I know not what you are,
Twinkle, twinkle, little star.

Notes

Listen for the rhyming pattern (prosody) of AABB.

The English lyrics were first written as a poem by Jane Taylor (1783–1824) and published with the title "The Star" in *Rhymes for the Nursery* by Jane and her sister Ann Taylor (1782–1866) in London.

This is a good poem to read in the winter when it is easy to view bright stars in the early dark of night.

Find: The stars that form the constellation Orion, the Hunter in the winter sky. You will likely see Venus, which is very bright, but a planet.

Book: *Henry and Mudge and the Starry Night* by Cynthia Rylant

Winter Birds
Anonymous

I can't go visit a snowbird
-I don't know where he stays.
I can't go visit a chickadee
-He has such flitty ways.
I can't go visit a blue jay
Atop a snowy tree,
And so I scatter seeds around
And have them visit ME.

Notes

Art tutorial: https://artprojectsforkids.org/winter-birch-trees/ use painter's tape & thin blue water color.

Activity: Scatter seeds on the ground near a window and watch birds visit the seeds to eat. You can also spread peanut butter on a pine cone or toilet paper tube, sprinkle seeds to stick to the peanut butter and tie outside with yarn.

Listen: for the sound of the chickadee bird in your yard; he says his name "chick-a-dee-dee-dee".

Activity: The Great Backyard Bird Count (2nd week in February). You can download a list of possible birds to notice in your vicinity at gbbc.birdcount.org.

Book: *Owl Moon* by Jane Yolen is a picture book that tells the story of a girl and her dad watching owls in the woods by the light of the moon.

February

Winter

How Do I Love Thee?

By Elizabeth Barrett Browning
England, 1845

How do I love thee? Let me count the ways.
I love thee to the depth and breadth and height
My soul can reach, when feeling out of sight
For the ends of being and ideal grace.
I love thee to the level of every day's
Most quiet need, by sun and candle-light.
I love thee freely, as men strive for right.
I love thee purely, as they turn from praise.
I love thee with the passion put to use
In my old griefs, and with my childhood's faith.
I love thee with a love I seemed to lose
With my lost saints. I love thee with the breath,
Smiles, tears, of all my life; and, if God choose,
I shall but love thee better after death.

Mrs. Browning lived from 1806 to 1861. She was a celebrated English poet of the Romantic Movement and knew other famous poets like William Wordsworth. This was written during her days of courtship with Robert Browning.

This poem is Sonnet 43 from a collection called "The Portuguese". A sonnet is a poem with 14 lines with 10 syllables in each line.

Map: Find England, where the author was born.

Visit in person or online: The Armstrong-Browning Library at Baylor University in Waco, Texas. It has a large collection of personal objects belonging to Mr. and Mrs. Browning.

I Corinthians 13:4-8

By the word of the Lord through Paul, the apostle
Ephesus, 55

Charity suffereth long, and is kind;
charity envieth not;
charity vaunteth not itself,
is not puffed up,
Doth not behave itself unseemly,
seeketh not her own,
is not easily provoked,
thinketh no evil;
Rejoiceth not in iniquity,
but rejoiceth in the truth;
Beareth all things,
believeth all things,
hopeth all things,
endureth all things.
Charity never faileth:
but whether there be prophecies, they shall fail;
whether there be tongues, they shall cease;
whether there be knowledge, it shall vanish away.

Notes

While this scripture does not rhyme and is not poetry, it is poetic and memorable like poetry. Memorize this passage from Corinthians; younger children can remember I John 4:8 God is Love.

Holiday: February 14 is Valentine's Day, which is a day to think about love.

Map: Paul was in Ephesus (in modern day Turkey) when he wrote to the Corinthians in Greece

Clouds

By Christina Rossetti
England, 19th Century

White sheep, white sheep,
On a blue hill,
When the wind stops
You all stand still
When the wind blows
You walk away slow.
White sheep, white sheep,
Where do you go?

Notes

Miss Rossetti liked to write about nature.

Look for clouds in winter and spring.
Art: paint clouds in dark blue water colors, let dry, then set outside to get wet again by a light rain; let dry again before using paper for wrapping, cards, or bookmarks.

Books: *Clouds* by Anne Rockwell (Lets-Read-and-find-out-about-Science series). *The Little Lamb* by Judy Dunn. Older Children can look for the water cycle described in the poem "Clouds" by Percy Byss Shelly, read the picture book *The Man Who Named Clouds* by Julie Hanna about Luke Howard, and research John Constable, the landscape painter that studied clouds.

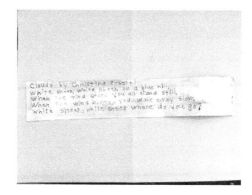

Eulogy to George Washington

By Henry "Light Horse Harry" Lee
America, 1799

First in war, first in peace, and first in the hearts of his countrymen, he was second to none in the humble and endearing scenes of private life. Pious, just, humane, temperate, and sincere; uniform, dignified, and commanding, his example was as edifying to all around him as were the effects of that example lasting. To his equals he was condescending, to his inferiors kind, and to the dear object of his affections exemplarily tender. Correct throughout, vice shuddered in his presence, and virtue always felt his fostering hand. The purity of his private character gave effulgence to his public virtues.

Notes

This is a good excerpt to read the third week of February to remember George Washington's birthday, February 22, 1732. The birthday is celebrated as a National holiday in America on the third Monday of the month.

George Washington was the first elected President of America. To celebrate him in 1862, President Abraham Lincoln recommended that people celebrate Washington's Birthday with public readings of Washington's Farewell Address from 1796.

About the author of this passage: George Washington passed on December 26, 1799. General Lee delivered a long funeral oration about Washington before the two Houses of Congress, which were meeting at Philadelphia, Pennsylvania. Lee was a major general in the Continental Army under Washington, a member of the Continental Congress, a governor of Virginia, father of the famous Civil War general Robert E. Lee, and close friend of George Washington.

Bake: Washington liked Cherry Pie and grew cherries at Mount Vernon. Mount Vernon's website has a reliable recipe.

Art: tutorials for Washington's likeness can be found https://artprojectsforkids.org/how-to-draw-george-washington-step-by-step/ and https://www.chalkpastel.com/product/american-history-video-art-lessons/.

Art: Look at a quarter coin! That image was based on a painting by American artist Gilbert Stuart, for whom Washington posed.

March

Spring

I Wandered Lonely as a Cloud

By William Wordsworth,
England, 1807

I wandered lonely as a cloud
That floats on high o'er vales and hills,
When all at once I saw a crowd,
A host, of golden daffodils;
Beside the lake, beneath the trees,
Fluttering and dancing in the breeze.

Continuous as the stars that shine
And twinkle on the milky way,
They stretched in never-ending line
Along the margin of a bay:
Ten thousand saw I at a glance,
Tossing their heads in sprightly dance.

The waves beside them danced; but they
Out-did the sparkling waves in glee:
A poet could not but be gay,
In such a jocund company:
I gazed—and gazed—but little thought
What wealth the show to me had brought:

For oft, when on my couch I lie
In vacant or in pensive mood,
They flash upon that inward eye
Which is the bliss of solitude;
And then my heart with pleasure fills,
And dances with the daffodils.

Notes

Depending on where you live, you will see daffodils in early spring around the second week of March, announcing that spring is coming.

Wordsworth wrote this poem two years after he experienced it during a vacation in the Lake District of England (his sister wrote about this day in her journal too!). Wordsworth liked to write about memories and nature. He lived 1770-1850 (His birthday is in April).

Vocabulary: "Jocund" means cheerful, "Pensive" describes serious thought.

Prosody: 8 syllables each line. Listen for rhyming pattern: ABABCC.

Literary Device: Empathy is feeling the same feeling as another, as in "wandered lonely as a cloud" or "dances with the daffodils"; Simile is a comparison using the words like or as, as in "I Wandered Lonely As a Cloud"; Hyperbole is exaggeration, as in "ten-thousand saw I at a glance"; Personification is a attributing human characteristics to a non-human, as in "Tossing their heads in sprightly dance".

Art: https://artprojectsforkids.org/draw-daffodil/

A place for everything

By Samuel Smiles
Scotland, 1875

A place for everything and
everything in its place.
I put my things away
that I might find them another day.

Notes

This Victorian maxim appears in the *McGuffey Readers*.
Benjamin Franklin liked to reference it also. This easy to say
poem pre-dates all the modern organizing books and theories!

This poem can be read any time of year, especially during Spring
Cleaning; spring is a good time to learn new habits.

Prayer of St. Patrick

By Patrick,
Ireland, 433

As I arise today,
may the strength of God pilot me,
the power of God uphold me,
the wisdom of God guide me.
May the eye of God look before me,
the ear of God hear me,
the word of God speak for me.
May the hand of God protect me,
the way of God lie before me,
the shield of God defend me,
the host of God save me.

May Christ shield me today.
Christ with me, Christ before me,
Christ behind me,
Christ in me, Christ beneath me,
Christ above me,
Christ on my right, Christ on my left,
Christ when I lie down, Christ when I sit, Christ when I stand,
Christ in the heart of everyone who thinks of me,
Christ in the mouth of everyone who speaks of me,
Christ in every eye that sees me,
Christ in every ear that hears me.
Amen.

Notes

Some people celebrate St. Patrick during the third week of March. On March 17, 461, the Christian missionary Patrick died in Ireland. Born to a wealthy Roman family, Patrick was captured and sold into slavery at 16. After six years, he was able to get home to England. After studying for the priesthood, he returned to Ireland where he spent 40 years preaching the gospel of Jesus.

In 433 A.D., history tells us that Patrick was praying for God's divine protection in his work and ministry in Ireland while facing powerful enemies. He wrote this prayer called St. Patrick's Breastplate, which is still widely known and recited today. God soon opened the door for him to share Christ with the Irish King Laoghaire and his subjects, and allowed him to be a part of bringing them out of paganism's dark hold to the saving power of Jesus Christ. Patrick was a man who knew much about darkness, hardship, and enemy territory.

Bible Verse: "For the Lord God is a sun and shield; the Lord bestows favor and honor; no good thing does He withhold from those who walk uprightly." Ps. 84:11

Art: https://artprojectsforkids.org/?s=shamrock
(extra supplies--gold paint pen)

Books: *The Story of Saint Patrick* by James Janda *and Across A Dark and Wild Sea* by Don Brown (about Columcille, Christian missionary to Scotland)

Easter

By Edmund Spenser
England, 1595

MOST glorious Lord of Lyfe! that, on this day,
Didst make Thy triumph over death and sin;
And, having harrowd hell, didst bring away
Captivity thence captive, us to win:
This joyous day, deare Lord, with joy begin;
And grant that we, for whom thou diddest dye,
Being with Thy deare blood clene washt from sin,
May live for ever in felicity!

And that Thy love we weighing worthily,
May likewise love Thee for the same againe;
And for Thy sake, that all lyke deare didst buy,
With love may one another entertayne!
So let us love, deare Love, lyke as we ought,
--Love is the lesson which the Lord us taught.

Notes

This is one sonnet from a longer work, "Amoretti". Look for the rhyme scheme ABABBCBC CDCDEE, devised by the author. A sonnet is an English poem of fourteen lines typically having ten syllables per line.

Further Study: Older students can read the 16th century epic English poem by Spenser "The Faerie Queen" with its ships and knights.

Dates: The date for the Easter commemoration varies by four weeks. You can read this poem in March or April depending on the year. Commonly, Easter Sunday is the first Sunday, after the first full moon, after the Vernal Equinox.

Art: https://www.hodgepodge.me/easter-cross-chalk-art-tutorial/

April

Spring

Work While You Work

By Author unknown

Work while you work,
Play while you play,
This is the way
To be happy each day.

All that you do,
Do with your might,
Things done by half
Are never done right.

McGuffey wrote his readers for an American audience. He thought poetry was important enough to alternate with prose, every other lesson.

It is a rhythmic poem to learn to recite while working. It inspires my son to focus on work not play when it was time to work, not play! Spring has many opportunities for duty before leisure.

The Bible supports the sentiment: Ecclesiastes 3:1 "To everything there is a season, and a time to every purpose under the heaven…." and Ecclesiastes 9:10 "Whatsoever thy hand findeth to do, do it with thy might…."

Rain

By Robert Louis Stevenson
Scotland, 1885

The rain is raining all around,
It falls on field and tree,
It rains on the umbrellas here,
And on the ships at sea.

Notes

Listen for the rhyming pattern ABCB; the rhyming pattern in poetry is called "prosody".

Robert Louis Stevenson was a Scottish poet that lived from 1850 to 1894. He traveled to many places including America. He is famous for writing books for adults like Treasure Island.

This is a good poem to learn during the spring rainy season.

Books: *Rabbits and Raindrops* by Jim Arnosky, (good writer and a good illustrator) and *In which Piglet is Entirely Surrounded by Water* by A.A. Milne.

Paul Revere's Ride

By Henry Wadsworth Longfellow
America, 1861

Listen, my children, and you shall hear
Of the midnight ride of Paul Revere,
On the eighteenth of April, in Seventy-Five:
Hardly a man is now alive
Who remembers that famous day and year.

He said to his friend, "If the British march
By land or sea from the town to-night,
Hang a lantern aloft in the belfry-arch
Of the North-Church-tower, as a signal-light,—
One if by land, and two if by sea;
And I on the opposite shore will be,
Ready to ride and spread the alarm
Through every Middlesex village and farm,
For the country-folk to be up and to arm."

Then he said "Good night!" and with muffled oar
Silently rowed to the Charlestown shore,
Just as the moon rose over the bay,
Where swinging wide at her moorings lay
The Somerset, British man-of-war:
A phantom ship, with each mast and spar
Across the moon, like a prison-bar,
And a huge black hulk, that was magnified
By its own reflection in the tide.

Meanwhile, his friend, through alley and street
Wanders and watches with eager ears,
Till in the silence around him he hears
The muster of men at the barrack door,
The sound of arms, and the tramp of feet,
And the measured tread of the grenadiers   (continued)

Marching down to their boats on the shore.

Then he climbed to the tower of the church,
Up the wooden stairs, with stealthy tread,
To the belfry-chamber overhead,
And startled the pigeons from their perch
On the sombre rafters, that round him made
Masses and moving shapes of shade,—
By the trembling ladder, steep and tall,
To the highest window in the wall,
Where he paused to listen and look down
A moment on the roofs of the town,
And the moonlight flowing over all.

Beneath, in the churchyard, lay the dead,
In their night-encampment on the hill,
Wrapped in silence so deep and still
That he could hear, like a sentinel's tread,
The watchful night-wind, as it went
Creeping along from tent to tent,
And seeming to whisper, "All is well!"
A moment only he feels the spell
Of the place and the hour, and the secret dread
Of the lonely belfry and the dead;
For suddenly all his thoughts are bent
On a shadowy something far away,
Where the river widens to meet the bay,—
A line of black, that bends and floats
On the rising tide, like a bridge of boats.

Meanwhile, impatient to mount and ride,
Booted and spurred, with a heavy stride,
On the opposite shore walked Paul Revere.
Now he patted his horse's side,
Now gazed on the landscape far and near,
Then impetuous stamped the earth,   (continued)

44

And turned and tightened his saddle-girth;
But mostly he watched with eager search
The belfry-tower of the old North Church,
As it rose above the graves on the hill,
Lonely and spectral and sombre and still.
And lo! as he looks, on the belfry's height,
A glimmer, and then a gleam of light!
He springs to the saddle, the bridle he turns,
But lingers and gazes, till full on his sight
A second lamp in the belfry burns!

A hurry of hoofs in a village-street,
A shape in the moonlight, a bulk in the dark,
And beneath from the pebbles, in passing, a spark
Struck out by a steed that flies fearless and fleet:
That was all! And yet, through the gloom and the light,
The fate of a nation was riding that night;
And the spark struck out by that steed, in his flight,
Kindled the land into flame with its heat.

He has left the village and mounted the steep,
And beneath him, tranquil and broad and deep,
Is the Mystic, meeting the ocean tides;
And under the alders, that skirt its edge,
Now soft on the sand, now loud on the ledge,
Is heard the tramp of his steed as he rides.

It was twelve by the village clock
When he crossed the bridge into Medford town.
He heard the crowing of the cock,
And the barking of the farmer's dog,
And felt the damp of the river-fog,
That rises when the sun goes down.

It was one by the village clock,
When he galloped into Lexington.   (continued)

45

He saw the gilded weathercock
Swim in the moonlight as he passed,
And the meeting-house windows, blank and bare,
Gaze at him with a spectral glare,
As if they already stood aghast
At the bloody work they would look upon.

It was two by the village clock,
When be came to the bridge in Concord town.
He heard the bleating of the flock,
And the twitter of birds among the trees,
And felt the breath of the morning breeze
Blowing over the meadows brown.
And one was safe and asleep in his bed
Who at the bridge would be first to fall,
Who that day would be lying dead,
Pierced by a British musket-ball.

You know the rest. In the books you have read,
How the British Regulars fired and fled,—
How the farmers gave them ball for ball,
From behind each fence and farmyard-wall,
Chasing the red-coats down the lane,
Then crossing the fields to emerge again
Under the trees at the turn of the road,
And only pausing to fire and load.

So through the night rode Paul Revere;
And so through the night went his cry of alarm
To every Middlesex village and farm,—
A cry of defiance, and not of fear,
A voice in the darkness, a knock at the door,
And a word that shall echo forevermore!
For, borne on the night-wind of the Past,
Through all our history, to the last,
In the hour of darkness and peril and need,   (continued)

The people will waken and listen to hear
The hurrying hoof-beats of that steed,
And the midnight message of Paul Revere.

Notes

Henry Wadsworth Longfellow lived from 1807 to 1882. Even though this poem was written at the time of the American Civil War, it commemorates the actions of American patriot Paul Revere on April 18, 1775 at the start of the American Revolutionary War with England.

You can read this poem in picture book form for children from several different illustrators.

Younger children can learn the first stanza by heart and write it on a bookmark designed to look like a lantern. Older students can study further by comparing the poem with the actual events.

Hamlet

By William Shakespeare
England, 1601

To be, or not to be, that is the question,
Whether 'tis nobler in the mind to suffer
The slings and arrows of outrageous fortune,
Or to take arms against a sea of troubles,
And by opposing end them? To die: to sleep;
No more; and by a sleep to say we end
The heart-ache and the thousand natural shocks
That flesh is heir to, 'tis a consummation
Devoutly to be wish'd. To die, to sleep;
To sleep: perchance to dream: ay, there's the rub;
For in that sleep of death what dreams may come
When we have shuffled off this mortal coil,
Must give us pause: there's the respect
That makes calamity of so long life;
For who would bear the whips and scorns of time,
The oppressor's wrong, the proud man's contumely,
The pangs of despised love, the law's delay,
The insolence of office and the spurns
That patient merit of the unworthy takes,
When he himself might his quietus make
With a bare bodkin? who would fardels bear,
To grunt and sweat under a weary life,
But that the dread of something after death,
The undiscover'd country from whose bourn
No traveller returns, puzzles the will
And makes us rather bear those ills we have
Than fly to others that we know not of?
Thus conscience does make cowards of us all;
And thus the native hue of resolution
Is sicklied o'er with the pale cast of thought,
And enterprises of great pith and moment
With this regard their currents turn awry,   (continued)

And lose the name of action.—Soft you now!
The fair Ophelia! Nymph, in thy orisons
Be all my sins remember'd.

Notes

This is a good excerpt to read the third week in April because
William Shakespeare was born April 23, 1564. To celebrate
Shakespeare's birthday your family could cook Old English
food, like a pasty, or meat pie eaten out of hand. Each child could
recite a line from Shakespeare: a toddler could say "Rosemary
for Remembrance", middle children could recite words invented
by Shakespeare and older children could read or recite a
soliloquy.

This excerpt of a soliloquy comes from William Shakespeare's
play "Hamlet" and is spoken by the Prince Hamlet in Act 3,
Scene 1, who is contemplating life. A "soliloquy" is speaking
one's thoughts aloud when alone, especially by a character in a
play.

Book for older readers: *Coined by Shakespeare: Words and
Meanings First Penned by the Bard* by Stanley Malless

May

Spring

The White Kitten

from McGuffey's Third Reader of the Eclectic Series
America, 1879

My little white kitten's asleep on my knee;
As white as the snow or the lilies is she;
She wakes up with a purr
When I stroke her soft fur:
Was there ever another white kitten like her?

My little white kitten now wants to go out
And frolic, with no one to watch her about;
"Little kitten," I say,
"Just an hour you may stay,
And be careful in choosing your places to play."

But night has come down, when I hear a loud "mew;"
I open the door, and my kitten comes through;
My white kitten! ah me!
Can it really be she—
This ill-looking, beggar-like cat that I see?

What ugly, gray streaks on her side and her back!
Her nose, once as pink as a rosebud, is black!
Oh, I very well know,
Though she does not say so,
She has been where white kittens ought never to go.

If little good children intend to do right,
If little white kittens would keep themselves white,
It is needful that they
Should this counsel obey,
And be careful in choosing their places to play.

Listen for the rhyme scheme or prosody of AABBB.

This was one of my older son's favorite poems in all of McGuffey's. Mr. William Holmes McGuffey wrote a series of books to teach children how to read. His stories were carefully chosen to include good examples of morality for children, like being obedient.

This poem can be read any time of year.

Book: *The Little Kitten* by Judy and Phoebe Dunn

The Children's Hour

By Henry Wadsworth Longfellow,
America, 1860

Between the dark and the daylight,
When the night is beginning to lower,
Comes a pause in the day's occupations,
That is known as the Children's Hour.

I hear in the chamber above me
The patter of little feet,
The sound of a door that is opened,
And voices soft and sweet.

From my study I see in the lamplight,
Descending the broad hall stair,
Grave Alice, and laughing Allegra,
And Edith with golden hair.

A whisper, and then a silence:
Yet I know by their merry eyes
They are plotting and planning together
To take me by surprise.

A sudden rush from the stairway,
A sudden raid from the hall!
By three doors left unguarded
They enter my castle wall!

They climb up into my turret
O'er the arms and back of my chair;
If I try to escape, they surround me;
They seem to be everywhere.

(continued)

53

They almost devour me with kisses,
Their arms about me entwine,
Till I think of the Bishop of Bingen
 In his Mouse-Tower on the Rhine!

Do you think, O blue-eyed banditti,
Because you have scaled the wall,
Such an old mustache as I am
Is not a match for you all!

I have you fast in my fortress,
And will not let you depart,
But put you down into the dungeon
In the round-tower of my heart.

And there will I keep you forever,
Yes, forever and a day,
Till the walls shall crumble to ruin,
And moulder in dust away!

Notes

Listen for the rhyming pattern, or prosody, or ABCB.

This is a good poem to read in the warm weather when that last hour of day is cool enough to enjoy out of doors before bedtime. This poem describes the poet's idyllic family life with his own three daughters playing in the garden around him.

Literary devices: The "blue-eyed banditti" is a metaphor referring to the author's daughters as robbers. The allusion, or passing reference, to "Bishop of Bingen, In his Mouse-Tower on the Rhine", is too morbid to explain to your young children. But here, the author feels like the bishop in the folk tale who is covered with mice, which are the author's daughters. A happy picture.

Art: https://www.artforkidshub.com/how-to-draw-fireflies-in-a-jar/ (medium: marker, crayon, watercolor for background) or *https://www.hodgepodge.me/?s=fireflies* (chalk medium)

Try, Try, Again

Found in McGuffey's Fourth Reader of the Eclectic Series
America, 1879

'Tis a lesson you should heed,
Try, try again;
If at first you don't succeed,
Try, try again;
Then your courage should appear,
For if you will persevere,
You will conquer, never fear
Try, try again;

Once or twice, though you should fail,
Try, try again;
If you would at last prevail,
Try, try again;
If we strive, 'tis no disgrace
Though we do not win the race;
What should you do in the case?
Try, try again

If you find your task is hard,
Try, try again;
Time will bring you your reward,
Try, try again
All that other folks can do,
Why, with patience, should not you?
Only keep this rule in view:
Try, try again.

Notes

Listen for the rhyme scheme, or prosody, of ABABCCCB.

This was one of my younger son's favorite poems in all of *McGuffey's Fourth Reader*. The lesson encouraged my son to persevere. Mr. William Holmes McGuffey thought poetry was important to young readers, thus lessons alternated between prose and poetry.

"Courage" means resolution "Persevere" means to continue your efforts even if it is hard. "Conquer" means gain the victory. "Prevail" means to overcome. "Patience" means to tolerate delay without getting upset or to be constant in labor.

This poem can be read any time of the year.

A Cry to Arms

By Henry Timrod
America, 1861

Ho! woodsmen of the mountain side!
Ho! dwellers in the vales!
Ho! ye who by the chafing tide
Have roughened in the gales!
Leave barn and byre, leave kin and cot,
Lay by the bloodless spade;
Let desk, and case, and counter rot,
And burn your books of trade.

The despot roves your fairest lands;
And till he flies or fears,
Your fields must grow but armed bands,
Your sheaves be sheaves of spears!
Give up to mildew and to rust
The useless tools of gain;
And feed your country's sacred dust
With floods of crimson rain!

Come, with the weapons at your call --
With musket, pike, or knife;
He wields the deadliest blade of all
Who lightest holds his life.
The arm that drives its unbought blows
With all a patriot's scorn,
Might brain a tyrant with a rose,
Or stab him with a thorn.

(continued)

Does any falter? let him turn
To some brave maiden's eyes,
And catch the holy fires that burn
In those sublunar skies.
Oh! could you like your women feel,
And in their spirit march,
A day might see your lines of steel
Beneath the victor's arch.

What hope, O God! would not grow warm
When thoughts like these give cheer?
The Lily calmly braves the storm,
And shall the Palm-tree fear?
No! rather let its branches court
The rack that sweeps the plain;
And from the Lily's regal port
Learn how to breast the strain!

Ho! woodsmen of the mountain side!
Ho! dwellers in the vales!
Ho! ye who by the roaring tide
Have roughened in the gales!
Come! flocking gayly to the fight,
From forest, hill, and lake;
We battle for our Country's right,
And for the Lily's sake!

Notes

Listen for the rhyme scheme, or prosody, or ABABCDCD.

Vocabulary: The "Lilly" in this poem refers to the women (wives, daughter, mothers, sisters) at home. "Scorn" means a feeling that something is worthless.

This is a good poem to read the fourth week in May near Memorial Day, which is a holiday devoted to remembering the soldiers who died in the line of duty. Originally, Southern women used flowers to decorate the graves of the Union and Confederate soldiers during the Civil War. Later the holiday came to include fallen US soldiers from any war.

Henry Timrod lived 1828-1867 in South Carolina. He was the so-called poet laureate of the Confederacy. This poem is an example of martial poetry which inspired men to enlist in the Confederate army.

June

Summer

Engine, Engine, Number Nine

By Author unknown
America, 19C

Engine, engine, number nine,
Sliding down Chicago line;
When she's polished she will shine,
Engine, engine, number nine.

Notes

Many variations of the poem exist, along with a variety of picture books set to those variations. This is a short poem to recite when your family sees a train. Book: for older learners is Trains by John Hudson Tiner. This poem can be read any time of year.

Art: Draw a train.
https://www.insightteched.com/collections/frontpage/products/complete-a-sketch-123-digital-download

Or https://artprojectsforkids.org/how-to-make-a-simple-train-drawing/

Activity: When time allows ride a ride train like Texas State Railroad in Rusk, TX, Durango & Silverton Narrow Gauge Railroad in Colorado, or a kiddie train like Forest Park Miniature Railroad in Ft. Worth, TX

Trees

By Sergeant Joyce Kilmer
America, 1914

I think that I shall never see
A poem lovely as a tree.

A tree whose hungry mouth is prest
Against the earth's sweet flowing breast;

A tree that looks at God all day,
And lifts her leafy arms to pray;

A tree that may in Summer wear
A nest of robins in her hair;

Upon whose bosom snow has lain;
Who intimately lives with rain.

Poems are made by fools like me,
But only God can make a tree.

Notes

Listen for the rhyme scheme or prosody of AA.

Mr. Kilmer was a journalist and poet. This poem came from a book titled Trees and Other Poems. He liked to write about nature and God. He lived from 1886-1914.

This poem can be read anytime of year.

Art: draw a tree from the tutorial
https://artprojectsforkids.org/how-to-draw-a-tree/

Add a swing or animal, or shadow, or something that shows what you like about trees.

Book: *A Tree is Nice* by Janice May Udry.

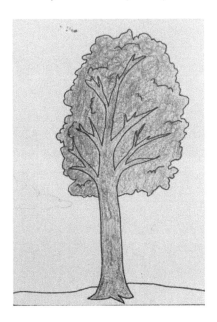

Sonnet 18

By William Shakespeare
England, 1608

Shall I compare thee to a summer's day?
Thou art more lovely and more temperate:
Rough winds do shake the darling buds of May,
And summer's lease hath all too short a date:
Sometime too hot the eye of heaven shines,
And often is his gold complexion dimm'd;
And every fair from fair sometime declines,
By chance, or nature's changing course, untrimm'd;
But thy eternal summer shall not fade
Nor lose possession of that fair thou ow'st;
Nor shall Death brag thou wander'st in his shade,
When in eternal lines to time thou grow'st;
So long as men can breathe or eyes can see,
So long lives this, and this gives life to thee.

Notes

This is a good sonnet to read in the summer because a summer day is described (depending on where you live, your day might not be so ideal)!

A sonnet is a verse form and has fourteen lines of iambic pentameter. Shakespeare's sonnets follow the pattern "abab cdcd efef gg". All the lines in iambic pentameter have five feet, consisting of an unstressed syllable followed by a stressed one.

William Shakespeare, 1564-1616, was an English poet, playwright and actor. He invented some words and wrote down some other words, already in use in speech, for the first time, like "Bandit", "Glow", and "Luggage".

To A Butterfly

By William Wordsworth
England, 1801

I've watched you now a full half-hour;
Self-poised upon that yellow flower
And, little Butterfly! indeed
I know not if you sleep or feed.
How motionless!--not frozen seas
More motionless! and then
What joy awaits you, when the breeze
Hath found you out among the trees,
And calls you forth again!

This plot of orchard-ground is ours;
My trees they are, my Sister's flowers;
Here rest your wings when they are weary;
Here lodge as in a sanctuary!
Come often to us, fear no wrong;
Sit near us on the bough!
We'll talk of sunshine and of song,
And summer days, when we were young;
Sweet childish days, that were as long
As twenty days are now.

Notes

This is a good poem to read in the summer when more butterflies are flying and feeding. Memorize the first stanza, then when you see a butterfly you will be ready to say your poem from heart.

William Wordsworth (1770-1850) lived in England and spent time with his sister when they were older; she wrote about this same incident in her own journal.

Art: Look for patterns of symmetry in live butterflies and photos. Follow a tutorial to draw a butterfly
https://artprojectsforkids.org/?s=butterfly
or use tracing paper to trace a picture in pencil, then turn the paper over and rub the lines with a pencil to transfer the image to blank paper. Look back at the picture to accurately color or paint the butterfly. Butterflies also make good outdoor photography subjects for young naturalists.

Activity: plant host plants in your garden to attract females to lay eggs. You will see the caterpillars feed on the host plant and then form a chrysalis. We often see the butterfly emerge after its metamorphosis; if not we often see the fresh butterfly fluttering about looking for nectar plants. Host plants include: Rue, Parsley, Dill, Fennel all for Swallowtails, Milkweed for Monarchs, Hollyhocks, Pansies for Painted Lady, and Passion vine for Gulf Fritillary.

Books: A well-illustrated book about the different varieties with lovely narrative is *A Butterfly Is Patient* by Dianna Aston and Sylvia Long. *Monarch Butterfly* by David M. Schwartz (Life Cycles series for younger children). *The Life Cycles of Butterflies: From egg to maturity, a visual guide to 23 common garden butterflies* by Judy Burris.

July

Summer

Declaration of Independence

By Thomas Jefferson
America, 1776

The unanimous Declaration of the thirteen united States of America,
When in the Course of human events, it becomes necessary for one people to dissolve the political bands which have connected them with another, and to assume among the powers of the earth, the separate and equal station to which the Laws of Nature and of Nature's God entitle them, a decent respect to the opinions of mankind requires that they should declare the causes which impel them to the separation.

We hold these truths to be self-evident, that all men are created equal, that they are endowed by their Creator with certain unalienable Rights, that among these are Life, Liberty and the pursuit of Happiness.--

That to secure these rights, Governments are instituted among Men, deriving their just powers from the consent of the governed, --That whenever any Form of Government becomes destructive of these ends, it is the Right of the People to alter or to abolish it, and to institute new Government, laying its foundation on such principles and organizing its powers in such form, as to them shall seem most likely to effect their Safety and Happiness.

Notes

This is just the introduction and beginning of the document read in Congress held in Philadelphia, Pennsylvania, July 4, 1776. For younger children, this passage will be more memorable if you stop at "the pursuit of Happiness." Older children can understand the next section.

This passage is not poetry, but it is poetic. It is good to read the first week of July because of Independence Day on July 4th.

Bed in Summer

By Robert Louis Stevenson
Scotland, 1885

In winter I get up at night
And dress by yellow candle-light.
In summer, quite the other way,
I have to go to bed by day.

I have to go to bed and see
The birds still hopping on the tree
Or hear the grown-up people's feet
Still going past me in the street.

And does it not seem hard to you,
When all the sky is clear and blue,
And I should like so much to play,
To have to go to bed by day?

Notes

Listen for the rhyme pattern (prosody) of AABB.

This poem was first published in *A Child's Garden of Verses*. Mr. Stevenson's noted for his book of poems for children, and books of fiction for adults like, *Treasure Island*. He also wrote about his travels!

This is a good poem to read any time in the summer, especially during Daylight Savings in the United States.

Sea Fever

By John Masefield
England, 1902

I must go down to the seas again, to the lonely sea and the sky,
And all I ask is a tall ship and a star to steer her by;
And the wheel's kick and the wind's song and the white sail's shaking,
And a grey mist on the sea's face, and a grey dawn breaking.

I must go down to the seas again, for the call of the running tide
Is a wild call and a clear call that may not be denied;
And all I ask is a windy day with the white clouds flying,
And the flung spray and the blown spume, and the sea-gulls crying.

I must go down to the seas again, to the vagrant gypsy life,
To the gull's way and the whale's way where the wind's like a whetted knife;
And all I ask is a merry yarn from a laughing fellow-rover,
And quiet sleep and a sweet dream when the long trick's over.

Notes

Listen for the rhyming pattern ABAB of the last word in each stanza of the poem.

Vocabulary: "Spume" means frothy foam. "Whetted" means sharp. "Yarn" is a long, hard to believe story. "Trick" is a turn at the wheel.

The author of "Sea Fever" was poet John Edward Masefield. He was born in 1878 in England and trained as a merchant seaman, who sailed on ships that traded goods for other people to buy. He worked other jobs before writing poems about his experience at sea. He followed good advice for all authors, "Write about what you know." He also wrote children's books. Later in life, Masefield was appointed British poet laureate in 1930 until his passing in 1967.

Books: Good picture books to read about the sea include *Beach Day* by Karen Roosa (a whole rhyming poem itself) and *The Maggie B* by Irene Haas (listen for the sister to sing to her little brother "Sweet and Low", a poem by Alfred, Lord Tennyson). Older children will enjoy *Swallows and Amazons* by Arthur Ransome and the true stories *Two Years Before the Mast* by Richard Henry Dana Jr.and *Carry On, Mr. Bowditch* by Jean Lee Latham.

General Store

By Rachel Field
America, 20th century

Someday I'm going to have a store
With a tinkly bell hung over the door,
With real glass cases and counters wide
And drawers all spilly with things inside.

There'll be a little of everything:
Bolts of calico; balls of string;
Jars of peppermint; tins of tea;
Pots and kettles; and crockery;

Seeds in packets; scissors bright;
Kegs of sugar, brown and white;
Sarsaparilla for picnic lunches,
Bananas and rubber boots in bunches.

I'll fix the window and dust each shelf,
And take the money in all myself,
It will be my store and I will say:
"What can I do for you today!"

Notes

Rachel Field (1894-1942) is also the author of popular books about American history: Calico Bush and Hitty, Her first 100 years.

Notice the rhyming pattern: AABB.

This poem can be read most any time of year, but especially if your kiddo opens a lemonade stand in the summer.

Art: Draw a store-front following this tutorial and then fill the window with what you sell! My children drew a bakery, a toy-store, and an antique shop (if you have a metallic colored pencil use it for the door hardware or window signage. https://artprojectsforkids.org/draw-a-shop/

Book: *Milly Molly Mandy* by Joyce Lankester Brisley (girls and boys will appreciate these stories).

August

Summer

What Do the Stars Do

By Christina Rossetti
England, 19th Century

What do the stars do
Up in the sky,
Higher than the wind can blow,
Or the clouds can fly?
Each star in its own glory
Circles, circles still;
As it was lit to shine and set,
And do its Maker's will.

Notes

Miss Rossetti was a member of a family of poets, writers, and artists.

Map: Find London on a map; it is the capital of England and where Miss Rossetti lived.

Art: Draw one constellation to recognize in each season on one side of your bookmark and list the brightest stars in the sky (and the constellations they are in and season to look for them) on the backside

Example:
Orion, Leo, Cygnus, Pegasus (in winter, spring, summer, autumn, respectively)

Sirius (Canis Major) in Winter
Arcturus (Bootes) in Spring
Vega (Lyra) in Fall
Capella (Auriga) Winter
Rigel (Orion) Winter

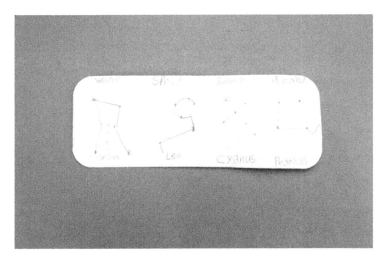

All Things Bright and Beautiful

By Cecil Frances Alexander
Ireland, 1848

All things bright and beautiful,
All creatures great and small,
All things wise and wonderful,
The Lord God made them all.

Each little flower that opens,
Each little bird that sings,
He made their glowing colours,
He made their tiny wings.

The rich man in his castle,
The poor man at his gate,
God made them, high or lowly,
And ordered their estate.

The purple-headed mountain,
The river running by,
The sunset, and the morning,
That brightens up the sky;

The cold wind in the winter,
The pleasant summer sun,
The ripe fruits in the garden,
He made them every one.

The tall trees in the greenwood,
The meadows where we play,
The rushes by the water,
We gather every day;--

(continued)

He gave us eyes to see them,
And lips that we might tell,
How great is God Almighty,
Who has made all things well

Notes

Sing: Mrs. Alexander wrote this poem as a hymn for children.
She started writing verse as a child! Later in life she helped the
poor and sick in Ireland.

Map: The author lived in Ireland; find it on a map.

Little Things

By Ebenezer Cobham Brewer
England, 19th century

Little drops of water,
Little grains of sand,
Make the mighty ocean
And the pleasant land.

Thus the little minutes,
Humble though they be,
Make the mighty ages
Of eternity.

So our little errors
Lead the soul away
From the path of virtue
Far in sin to stray.

Little deeds of kindness
Little words of love
Help to make earth happy
Like the heaven above.

Notes

Listen for the rhyming pattern (prosody) of ABCB.

The theme of this poem is timely in any season.

Art: A little bookmark with an ocean scene could have this poem written on the backside to keep it in front of your eyes. Or follow this tutorial https://artprojectsforkids.org/how-to-draw-a-sea-shell/ . To tie into the poem, sprinkle table salt on the wet watercolored water or sand background to emulate sand.

I'd Like to Be a Lighthouse

By Rachel Field
America, 19th century

I'd like to be a lighthouse
All scrubbed and painted white.
I'd like to be a lighthouse
And stay awake all night
To keep my eye on everything
That sails my patch of sea;
I'd like to be a lighthouse
With the ships all watching me.

Notes

Rachel Field had her first poem published when she was sixteen years old!

Art for older children: https://artprojectsforkids.org/edward-hopper-painting/ (and look at an image of the real painting by American artist Edward Hopper).

Art for younger children: https://artprojectsforkids.org/draw-a-lighthouse/

https://artprojectsforkids.org/how-to-draw-a-sailboat/

Book: *Little Red Lighthouse and the Great Gray Bridge* by Hildegard Swift (about a lighthouse and the George Washington Bridge on the Hudson River connecting New York City with New Jersey).

September

Autumn

Thirty Days hath September

By Mother Goose
England, 1590

Thirty Days hath September,
April, June, and November;
February has twenty-eight alone
All the rest have thirty-one
Except in Leap Year, that's the time
When February's Days are twenty-nine.

Notes

Variations of this poem exist from different historical sources. This Mother Goose version is based on a poem found in *Chronicles of England* by Richard Grafton, 1590.

September is an ideal month to learn this poem. Words used over the centuries for this season of the year: harvest, autumn, and fall.

Art "paint a fall landscape" from
https://artprojectsforkids.org/draw-a-fall-landscape/
This is a good lesson in perspective painting and fore-ground, middle ground, and background.

Book to read in the fall: *Mr. Putter and Tabby Pick the Pears* by Cynthia Rylant

Who Has Seen the Wind?

By Christina Rossetti
England. 19th Century

Who has seen the wind?
Neither I nor you:
But when the leaves hang trembling,
The wind is passing through.

Who has seen the wind?
Neither you nor I:
But when the trees bow down their heads,
The wind is passing by.

Notes

Christina Rossetti liked to write about nature and came from an artistic family. She lived in England from 1830-1894. Autumn is a good time to learn this poem because you will see the leaves falling from the wind blowing.

Art: falling leaves from the perspective of looking up at the tree (see bookmark example below)

Math moment: use leaves to begin learning about area as suggested in *Hug a Tree* by Robert Rockwell.

Book: *Autumn Leaves* by Ken Robbins

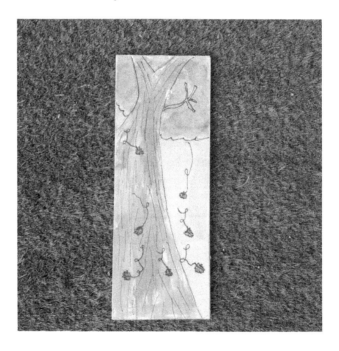

Preamble to United States Constitution

By James Madison
America, 1787

We the People of the United States, in Order to form a more
perfect Union, establish Justice, insure domestic Tranquility,
provide for the common defence, promote the general Welfare,
and secure the Blessings of Liberty to ourselves and our
Posterity, do ordain and establish this Constitution for the United
States of America.

Notes

This is the beginning of the US Constitution Signed in convention September 17, 1787, ratified June 21, 1788. It is lyrical and easy to memorize. In America, Constitution Day is September 17.

Read aloud the whole Constitution to your children at some point before they leave home as part of their civics education. Bank tellers are not taught the characteristics of counterfeit money, but are quizzed on the attributes of real money, so then; they can recognize the counterfeit bills.

Something Told the Wild Geese

By Rachel Field
America
20th Century

Something told the wild geese
It was time to go,
Though the fields lay golden
Something whispered, "snow."

Leaves were green and stirring,
Berries, luster-glossed,
But beneath warm feathers
Something cautioned, "frost."

All the sagging orchards
Steamed with amber spice,
But each wild breast stiffened
At remembered ice.

Something told the wild geese
It was time to fly,
Summer sun was on their wings,
Winter in their cry.

Notes

Ms. Field wrote many books for children, including *Prayer for a Child* (A Golden Book).

We chose this poem for September because when we watch geese pass over our home heading south, our memories are inspired to recite this heart-warming, seasonal poem in unison.

Art: https://artprojectsforkids.org/how-draw-a-basket-of-apples/ (satisfying as a colored pencil project)

Art: more challenging is to draw geese up close or as silhouettes in the sky. Jim Arnosky's *Sketching Outdoors in Autumn* provides nice art to copy.

Book*: Johnny Appleseed* by Reeve Lindbergh (geography, poem).

October

Autumn

Busy

By Phyllis Halloran
America, 20th century

Busy, busy, busy, busy,
Busy little squirrel --
Running, running, jumping,
In a dizzy whirl.
Stopping now and then to eat
A tasty little acorn treat –
Busy, busy, busy, busy,
Busy little squirrel.

Notes

Look for an illustration to this poem in Eric Carle's book *Animals, Animals* published in 1999. His medium is painted-paper collage.

Art: This poem will get recited regularly at the sight of a busy squirrel any time of year, especially during its fall preparations. The poem will fit on a bookmark with room for a squirrel drawing, which will take practice. Look for a 12-step tutorial online: "How to draw a squirrel" from Art for Kids Hub.

Books: *Every Autumn Comes the Bear* by Jim Arnosky (preparation for hibernation), *How the Forest Grew* by William Jaspersohn (look for examples in your own town of the red oak or live oak mentioned in the book).

In 1492

By Jean Marzollo
America, 1991

In fourteen hundred ninety-two
Columbus sailed the ocean blue.

He had three ships and left from Spain;
He sailed through sunshine, wind and rain.

He sailed by night; he sailed by day;
He used the stars to find his way.

A compass also helped him know
How to find the way to go.

Ninety sailors were on board;
Some men worked while others snored.

Then the workers went to sleep;
And others watched the ocean deep.

Day after day they looked for land;
They dreamed of trees and rocks and sand.

October 12 their dream came true,
You never saw a happier crew!

"Indians! Indians!" Columbus cried;
His heart was filled with joyful pride.

But "India" the land was not;
It was the Bahamas, and it was hot.

The Arakawa natives were very nice;
They gave the sailors food and spice.   (continued)

100

Columbus sailed on to find some gold
To bring back home, as he'd been told.

He made the trip again and again,
Trading gold to bring to Spain.

The first American? No, not quite.
But Columbus was brave, and he was bright.

Notes

This is a good poem for the second week of October because
Columbus Day in America is a holiday on the second Monday in
October. It celebrates the anniversary of Christopher Columbus'
arrival in the New World on October 12, 1492. His birthday is
also this month, October 31, 1451

Picture study: find an image of "The Carvels of Columbus"
painted by American artist NC Wyeth. Look at it for a long time,
then don't look at it and say what you remember. Look at it
again. Keep it visible all week. Remember five facts about it (one
for each finger). Who: NC Wyeth. What: "The Carvels of
Columbus". When: 20th Century (1927). Where (it can be seen
in person): National Geographic Headquarters in Washington,
DC. How: Oil on wall mural.

History: Your children can research the explorations of Vikings
(like Leif Erikson) and Scottish Monks (like Brennan and
Columcille aka Columba) before 1492.

Art tutorial https://www.hodgepodge.me/columbus-sailed-the-
ocean-blue-chalk-art-tutorial/

Book: *In 1492* by Jean Marzollo

Autumn Fires

By Robert Louis Stevenson
Scotland, 1885

In the other gardens
And all up the vale,
From the autumn bonfires
See the smoke trail!

Pleasant summer over
And all the summer flowers,
The red fire blazes,
The grey smoke towers.

Sing a song of seasons!
Something bright in all!
Flowers in the summer,
Fires in the fall!

Notes

The author, Mr. Stevenson lived from 1850-1894, mostly in Scotland, but he also traveled around the world looking for a climate that would improve his health. He finally found Samoa, an island in the Pacific Ocean.

This is a good poem to read anytime in fall.

Art: Have your children draw around a copy of this poem; expect the drawing to include a bonfire with smoke or a large leaf colored with a mixture of brown, yellow, red, and purple colored pencils (option: look around for fall colors in nature and then only have those choices of colors set out during drawing time) or https://artprojectsforkids.org/draw-a-fall-landscape/ (watercolor resist), or copy drawing below

Books: *The Year at Maple Hill Farm* by Alice and Martin Provensen, *Autumn Story* (Brambly Hedge series) by Jill Barklem (literary device: personification), *The Ox-cart man* by Donald Hall (themes of family, industry, seasonal cycle).

A Mighty Fortress Is Our God

By Martin Luther
Germany, ca.1529

A mighty fortress is our God, a bulwark never failing;
Our helper He, amid the flood of mortal ills prevailing:
For still our ancient foe doth seek to work us woe;
His craft and pow'r are great, and, armed with cruel hate,
On earth is not his equal.

Did we in our own strength confide, our striving would be losing,
Were not the right Man on our side, the Man of God's own
choosing:
Dost ask who that may be? Christ Jesus, it is He;
Lord Sabaoth, His Name, from age to age the same,
And He must win the battle.

And though this world, with devils filled, should threaten to undo
us,
We will not fear, for God hath willed His truth to triumph
through us;
The Prince of Darkness grim, we tremble not for him;
His rage we can endure, for lo, his doom is sure,
 One little word shall fell him.

That word above all earthly pow'rs, no thanks to them, abideth;
The Spirit and the gifts are ours through Him Who with us
sideth;
Let goods and kindred go, this mortal life also;
The body they may kill: God's truth abideth still,
His kingdom is forever.

Notes

This is a good poem to read at the end of October on Reformation Day. This holiday commemorates the day the German monk Martin Luther nailed his Ninety-five Theses on the door of the All Saints' Church in Wittenberg on 31 October 1517. He wanted to reform the church he loved so he wrote 95 statements about problems in the church that he wanted to debate.

Vocabulary: "bulwark" is a wall, person, or institution that provides defense.

Art: copy work from a fortress drawing in a book, similar to my son's drawing of a castle keep below.

Music: sing this song aloud or play on the piano using music from a church hymnal.

Related Bible verse: Psalm 18:2

November

Autumn

A Prayer to be Shared at Thanksgiving
By Jeanie Kilpatrick
America, 21st Century

Thank You, Father, for days full of sun,
For playtime and rest time and work to be done.

Thank You for beauty wherever we gaze,
For stars in the night, blue skies for the days.

Thank You for blessings that have no end,
The joy of a family, the love of a friend.

Thank You for health in our bodies and souls,
And for spirits that soar and never grow old.

Thank You for mercy that covers our sins,
Forgives our faults, makes us righteous again.

Thank You for grace that changes our ways,
And wisdom to walk with You all of our days.

Notes

Ms. Kilpatrick (1947-2010) was a school teacher, greeting card verse writer, and my mother in Texas. Thanksgiving was her favorite holiday, but this poem could be remembered any time of year when one wants to have a grateful heart.

Notice the rhyming scheme (prosody) is AABBCC....

Books of gratitude during this holiday season:
Plymouth Thanksgiving (If you only had time for one, pick this one, which my 6 year old loved.).
*N.C. Wyeth's Pilgrims_* (So wonderful; a favorite American artist.)
*Squanto and the Miracle of Thanksgiving_* by Eric Metaxas

Mayflower Compact
By William Bradford
Cape Cod, 1620

In the name of God, Amen. We whose names are under-written, the loyal subjects of our dread sovereign Lord, King James, by the grace of God, of Great Britain, France, and Ireland King, Defender of the Faith, etc.

Having undertaken, for the glory of God, and advancement of the Christian faith, and honor of our King and Country, a voyage to plant the first colony in the northern parts of Virginia, do by these presents solemnly and mutually, in the presence of God, and one of another, covenant and combine our selves together into a civil body politic, for our better ordering and preservation and furtherance of the ends aforesaid; and by virtue hereof to enact, constitute, and frame such just and equal laws, ordinances, acts, constitutions and offices, from time to time, as shall be thought most meet and convenient for the general good of the Colony, unto which we promise all due submission and obedience. In witness whereof we have hereunder subscribed our names at Cape Cod, the eleventh of November [New Style, November 21], in the year of the reign of our sovereign lord, King James, of England, France, and Ireland, the eighteenth, and of Scotland the fifty-fourth. Anno Dom. 1620.

Notes

This is a good writing to read the second week of November because it was originally signed on November 11th (November 21 in the new style, Julian calendar which was implemented in 1752).

The Separatists and Strangers, together called the Pilgrims, landed north of where they had permission from the King of England to settle as a colony of England. The permission was in the form of a charter. Some of the pilgrims questioned the authority of the leaders because of the new location not being previously approved by the King. Together the people on the Mayflower agreed on the form of government for the new settlement and signed this compact or contract. Research: Visit the Pilgrim Hall museum website to see all the names of the Pilgrims who signed this agreement. Pick one to read about in a book or in the encyclopedia.

Art: Draw the Mayflower https://artprojectsforkids.org/how-to-draw-a-ship/
To make this even more striking, use kraft scrapbooking paper (or brown paper bag) and draw the sails with a white colored pencil, red flags and black ink.

Book: *Stories of the Pilgrims* by Margaret Pumphrey (c. 1910) is a thorough and long read-aloud to start early so you can finish before the month of November. Bradford's Journal has been reprinted if you want to read a first person account.

Thanksgiving Day

By Lydia Maria Child
Massachusetts, 1844

Over the river, and through the wood,
To grandfather's house we go;
The horse knows the way
To carry the sleigh
Through the white and drifted snow.

Over the river, and through the wood—
Oh, how the wind does blow!
It stings the toes
And bites the nose
As over the ground we go.

Over the river, and through the wood,
To have a first-rate play.
Hear the bells ring
"Ting-a-ling-ding",
Hurrah for Thanksgiving Day!

Over the river, and through the wood
Trot fast, my dapple-gray!
Spring over the ground,
Like a hunting-hound!
For this is Thanksgiving Day.

Over the river, and through the wood,
And straight through the barn-yard gate.
We seem to go
Extremely slow,—
It is so hard to wait!

(continued)

Over the river and through the wood—
Now grandmother's cap I spy!
Hurrah for the fun!
Is the pudding done?
Hurrah for the pumpkin-pie!

Notes

Mrs. Child lived in New England from 1802-1880. Her brother made sure she had good books to read while she was growing up. As an adult she showed she cared about women, children, Indians, and slaves by writing about them and for them and giving money to people who helped them.

Notice this poem's rhyming pattern (prosody): ABCCB.

Vocabulary: "dapple-gray" is a color and pattern of horse.

Art: https://www.hodgepodge.me/fall-walk-in-the-woods-chalk-pastel-art-tutorial/

Art to study: find images to study (remember one fact for each finger on your hand--who painted, what is the title of the painting, when was it painted, where can you go see the original, how was it painted (medium used). "Catching the Turkey" by Grandma Moses (American Artist) and "Wild Turkey" by James John Audubon (American Artist)

(continued)

Books:

Over the River and Through the Woods (This is a board book for your Littles with art from woodcuts by Christopher Manson.)
1620: The Year of the Pilgrims (Includes what is going on around the world at the same time the Pilgrims are settling in the New World.)
An Old-Fashioned Thanksgiving by Louisa May Alcott (American Author, depicts 1881)
All About Turkeys by Jim Arnosky (animal studies)
Balloons over Broadway: The True Story of the Puppeteer of Macy's Parade (inventor, also watch video by History Channel about Macy's Day Parade in modern times)

Psalm 100
The Bible

Make a joyful noise unto the LORD, all ye lands.

Serve the LORD with gladness: come before his presence with singing.

Know ye that the LORD he is God: it is he that hath made us, and not we ourselves; we are his people, and the sheep of his pasture.

Enter into his gates with thanksgiving, and into his courts with praise: be thankful unto him, and bless his name.

For the Lord is good; his mercy is everlasting; and his truth endureth to all generations.

Notes

God had David write most of the Psalms, including this one. David lived from 1040 BC to 970 BC mostly in Jerusalem. He was the King of Israel and Judah. This is a good writing to read any time of year, but especially at Thanksgiving because it is a Psalm, or song, of gratitude to our Lord.

Memory Work: Assign each family member a verse in this Psalm, then recite it together--each person reciting their verse in turn (we say the last verse altogether). Your 3-4 year old can say the scripture reference or recite the first verse. This has something for everyone; parents or older kids can memorize more if needed. This is a blessing when recited to everyone gathered around the Thanksgiving table!

December

Winter

Christmas Everywhere

By Phillips Brooks
America, 1903

Everywhere, everywhere, Christmas tonight!
Christmas in lands of the fir-tree and pine,
Christmas in lands of the palm-tree and vine,
Christmas where snow peaks stand solemn and white,
Christmas where cornfields stand sunny and bright.
Christmas where children are hopeful and gay,
Christmas where old men are patient and gray,
Christmas where peace, like a dove in his flight,
Broods o're brave men in the thick of the fight;
Everywhere, everywhere, Christmas tonight!
For the Christ-child who comes is the Master of all;
No palace too great, no cottage too small.

Mr. Brooks was an Episcopal preacher in American and wrote the lyrics to the Christmas hymn, "O Little Town of Bethlehem". Anne Sullivan introduced him to Helen Keller. His wife was also deaf. Helen and Mr. and Mrs. Brooks talked and corresponded of the things of God and Helen asked that her newly born brother be named after Mr. Brooks.

Music and Scripture: You can follow instructions from Titus 2 ministries for a family Christmas program using scripture, hymns and tissue-wrapped nativity pieces to celebrate the events of Christ's birth in order. The program can be done in less than an hour with the whole family or a little each day for little ears for a week. https://titus2.com/christmas-program/

Book *A Christmas Carol* by Charles Dickens (Written in Victorian England in 1852, this tale from a famous author relates the story of repentance and redemption. Look for the gospel throughout the whole story ((for example: "God Rest you Merry Gentleman" carol, singing in honor of God, "the day people remember that they are on journey to grave", themes of Love your God and Love your neighbor, "A little child set before him", Timothy means full of God, "Saves", born again at the end.).. Sharpen your best Yorkshire accent and read aloud to the whole family.)

A Christmas Carol

By Christina Rossetti
England, 1872

What can I give Him,
Poor as I am?
If I were a shepherd
I would bring a lamb,
If I were a Wise Man
I would do my part,—
But what can I give Him?
I will give my heart.

Notes

This is a good poem to read in December because Christina Rossetti was born 5 December 1830 and passed 29 December 1894. This poem is the last stanza of a longer poem about the birth of Christ celebrated as Christmas in December.

Music: The poem was put to music by the famous composer Gustav Holst in 1906 and sung as the hymn "In the Bleak Midwinter".

Art: draw a wrapped present on the front and write this verse on the back for a bookmark or greeting card.

Books to read at Christmas time about giving:

Christmas in the Country by Cynthia Rylant & Diane Goode (two beloved authors and illustrators, this picture book relates the story of Ms. Rylant's childhood with her Grandparents.)

Christmas Day in the Morning by Pearl S. Buck (Ms. Buck was a notable adult author and Christian missionary to China from the Presbyterian Church.)

The Last Straw by Fredrick H. Thury. (Another picture book, this one a fictionalized account of a camel serving and worshipping the Christ child.)

Good King Wenceslas

By John Mason Neale
England, 1853

Good King Wenceslas look'd out,
On the Feast of Stephen;
When the snow lay round about,
Deep, and crisp, and even:
Brightly shone the moon that night,
Though the frost was cruel,
When a poor man came in sight,
Gath'ring winter fuel.

"Hither page and stand by me,
If thou know'st it, telling,
Yonder peasant, who is he?
Where and what his dwelling?"
"Sire, he lives a good league hence.
Underneath the mountain;
Right against the forest fence,
By Saint Agnes' fountain."

"Bring me flesh,and bring me wine,
Bring me pine-logs hither:
Thou and I will see him dine,
When we bear them thither."
Page and monarch forth they went,
Forth they went together;
Through the rudewind's wild lament,
And the bitter weather.

"Sire, the night is darker now,
And the wind blows stronger;
Fails my heart, I know now how,
I can go no longer."
"Mark my footsteps, good my page;

Tread thou in them boldly;
Thou shalt find the winter's rage
Freeze thy blood less coldly."

In his master's steps he trod,
Where the snow lay dinted;
Heat was in the very sod
Which the Saint had printed.
Therefore, Christian men, be sure,
Wealth or rank possessing,
Ye who now will bless the poor,
Shall yourselves find blessing.

Notes

This poem is based on a good deed by Wenceslaus, Duke of Bohemia, who lived from 907 to 935 AD. This story is a good example of discipleship, encouragement and a righteous king (*rex iustus*). This is a good poem to read the third week of December because the Feast of Stephen is on December 26.

Vocabulary: Hither means here, Thither means there

Find on a Map: Bohemia was part of modern day Czech Republic.

Music: Sing as a carol.

Book to read about another Godly man helping the poor: *Mommy, Was Santa Claus Born on Christmas Too?* by Barbara Knoll. (A narrative version for children of the historical relationship between Nicholas the Bishop and the Americanized Santa Claus.)

A Friend's Greeting

by Edgar Guest
America, 20th Century

I'd like to be the sort of friend that you have been to me;
I'd like to be the help that you've been always glad to be;
I'd like to mean as much to you each minute of the day
As you have meant, old friend of mine, to me along the way.

I'd like to do the big things and the splendid things for you,
To brush the gray from out your skies and leave them only blue;
I'd like to say the kindly things that I so oft have heard,
And feel that I could rouse your soul the way that mine you've
stirred.

I'd like to give you back the joy that you have given me,
Yet that were wishing you a need I hope will never be;
I'd like to make you feel as rich as I, who travel on
Undaunted in the darkest hours with you to lean upon.

I'm wishing at this Christmas time that I could but repay
A portion of the gladness that you've strewn along my way;
And could I have one wish this year, this only would it be:
I'd like to be the sort of friend that you have been to me.

Notice the rhyming scheme (prosody) of AABB.

Edgar Guest (1881–1959) was born in England and moved to America with his parents. He worked for a newspaper in Detroit, Michigan for sixty-five years beginning at age 14 as a copy boy and working his way to the news department. He said about his own poetry, "I take simple everyday things that happen to me and I figure it happens to a lot of other people and I make simple rhymes out of them."

This is a good poem to read anytime around Christmas time. And a good one to write to a friend, maybe with a watercolor painting of seasonal fir trees.

Art: watercolor fir trees with a regular brush or https://stepbysteppainting.net/2018/06/18/painting-trees-with-a-fan-brush/

Book: Robert Frost's *Stopping by Woods on a Snowy Evening* poem, illustrated by Susan Jeffers (illustrations set the poem before Christmas).

Planning

January
The North Wind Doth Blow by Mother Goose (anytime in winter) p. 12
Snow by Alice Wilkins (anytime in winter) p. 14
Twinkle, Twinkle, Little Star by Jane Taylor (anytime) p. 16
Winter Birds by Anonymous (anytime in winter) p.18

February
How Do I Love Thee? by Browning (anytime, especially near Valentine's Day) p.21
I Corinthians 13:4-8 from the Bible (anytime, especially near Valentine's Day) p.23
Clouds by Christina Rossetti (anytime) p.25
George Washington's Eulogy by Lee (Washington's Birthday February 22, 1732) p.27

March
I Wandered Lonely As a Cloud by Wordsworth (early spring when Daffodils blooming) p.30
A Place for Everything from Victorian saying (anytime) p.32
St. Patrick's Breastplate by Patrick (Patrick's Day, historical date died March 17, 461 AD) p.34
Easter by Edmund Spenser (March or April, depending on the moveable date of Easter) p.36

April
Work While You Work (anytime) p.39
Rain by Robert Louis Stevenson (anytime it is rainy season) p.41
Paul Revere's Ride by Longfellow (historical date April 18, 1775) p.43
Hamlet by William Shakespeare (anytime, Shakespeare's birthday April 23, 1564) p.48

May
White Kitten from McGuffey's Reader (anytime) p.51
Children's Hour by Wadsworth (anytime) p.53
Try, Try, Again by Hickson (anytime) p.56
A Cry to Arms by Timrod (Memorial Day) p.58

June
Engine, Engine, Number Nine (anytime) p.62
Trees by Kilmer (anytime, "summer" & "snow" are in the text) p.64
Sonnet 18 by William Shakespeare (anytime in summer, "summer" is in the text) p.66
To A Butterfly by Wordsworth (any season with butterflies, "summer" is in the text) p.68

July
Declaration of Independence by Jefferson (July 4, 1774) p.71
Bed in Summer by Robert Louis Stevenson (anytime in summer) p.73
Sea Fever by John Mansfield (anytime) p.75
General Store by Rachel Field (anytime) p.77

August
What Do the Stars Do by Christina Rossetti (anytime) p.80
All Things Bright and Beautiful by Alexander (anytime, "winter" and "summer" are in the text) p.82
Little Things by Ebenezer Cobham Brewer (anytime) p.84
Lighthouse by Rachel Field (anytime) p.86

September
30 days hath September by Mother Goose (anytime in September) p.89
Who has Seen the Wind by Christina Rossetti (anytime) p.91
Preamble to the Constitution by Madison (Constitution Day, Historical date September 17, 1787) p.93

Something told the wild Geese by Field (anytime in autumn) p.95

October
Busy, Busy Squirrel by Phyllis Halloran (anytime) p.98
Columbus Sailed the Ocean Blue in 1492 by Marzollo (Columbus Day, historical Date October 12, 1492) p.100
Autumn Fires by Robert Louis Stevenson (anytime in autumn) p.102
A Mighty Fortress is Our God by Luther (Reformation Day, historical date October 31, 1517) p.104

November
A Prayer to be Shared at Thanksgiving (anytime) p.107
Mayflower Compact by William Bradford (Historical date November 11, 1620) p.109
Thanksgiving Day by Child (Thanksgiving Day) p.111
Psalm 100 by David (anytime) p.114

December
Christmas Everywhere by Phillips Brooks (Anytime in December) p.117
A Christmas Carol by Rossetti (Anytime in December) p.119
Good King Wenceslas by John Mason Neale (especially near December 26) p.121
A Friend by Edgar Guest (Anytime in December) p.123

Made in the USA
Las Vegas, NV
28 March 2021

20342929R00080